ANCIENT EGYPT: PYRAMIDS AND PHARAOHS

SPEEDY
PUBLISHING

Speedy Publishing LLC
40 E. Main St. #1156
Newark, DE 19711
www.speedypublishing.com

Ancient Egypt was a thriving civilization, lasting over 3,000 years.

Ancient Egyptian pyramids are the most well known pyramid structures. There are around 138 Egyptian pyramids.

Most Ancient Egyptian pyramids were built as tombs for Pharaohs and their families.

The pyramids of Egypt are all built to the west of the Nile River. This is because the western side was associated with the land of the dead.

The Pharaohs of Ancient Egypt were the supreme leaders of the land.

A Pharaoh was the most important and powerful person in the kingdom.

The Pharaohs wore a crown that had an image of the cobra goddess. Only the Pharaoh was allowed to wear the cobra goddess.

Pharaohs built great tombs for themselves so they could live well in the afterlife.

Made in United States
Orlando, FL
08 March 2023